The Missing

The True Story of
My Family in World War II

For **Emma**, **Elsie** and **Emile**.
In memory of my father's
"missing" uncles and aunts:
Oscar (Jeschie) and **Rachel**, **Martin**,
Stella and **Bernard**, **Bella**, **Willi** and **Genia**.

This book is supported and checked by the
UCL Centre for Holocaust Education.

First published 2019 by Walker Books Ltd
87 Vauxhall Walk, London SE11 5HJ

This edition published 2021

2 4 6 8 10 9 7 5 3 1

Text © 2019 Michael Rosen

The right of Michael Rosen to be identified as author of this work
has been asserted by him in accordance with the Copyright, Designs
and Patents Act 1988

This book has been typeset in Clarendon T

Printed and bound by CPI Group (UK) Ltd, Croydon CR0 4YY

British Library cataloguing in Publication Data: a catalogue record for this
book is available from the British Library

ISBN 978-1-4063-9559-4

www.walker.co.uk

FSC
MIX
Paper
FSC® C101537

MICHAEL ROSEN

The Missing

The True Story of My Family in World War II

WALKER BOOKS

Not Just For Them

This is about France.

This is about Germany.

This is about Jews.

This is not about France.

This is not about Germany.

This is not about Jews.

This story is about things that happened to my family a long time ago, back when photos and films were in black and white. But when I think about it, my relatives were refugees – a lot like the people you may have seen on the news recently.

Because of the events of the Second World War, they were forced to run: to flee and hide. When I turn on the TV now, eighty years later, I see thousands of families that have been forced to run from new wars, driven into hiding and sometimes losing their lives.

So I hope this book becomes part of a bigger conversation about the refugee crisis. About how to find fair and decent ways of helping people like my relatives.

Michael Rosen

INTRODUCTION

I was born in 1946, the year after the Second World War ended.

You probably know about the war already: that a group of countries called the "Axis powers" were fighting another group of countries called the "Allies".

You probably also know that Nazi Germany was one of the Axis powers, along with Italy and Japan. And that Britain was one of the Allies – which, by the end of the war, also included the USA and the Soviet Union.

I expect you know that the Allies won in the end. I was born exactly nine months after Allied troops led a victory parade through the ruins of Berlin.

And I'm sure you know that lots of people died during the war – and not just on the battlefields.

Throughout my childhood, I didn't know whether my relatives were among them. Stories used to hang in the air about French and Polish great-aunts and great-uncles, who were there before the war and weren't after.

What happened? I'd ask.

Don't know, my family would say.

And it was true: they genuinely didn't know. It didn't make any sense to me... How could people just disappear like that? People with whole lives? People with families who loved them?

So, over many years, I tried to find out exactly what happened. The search took me to several different countries and this book is the result.

I've included poems, too, written over the years. They're about what happened to my relatives, and how I felt about the things I found out. Poems are like special rooms where I can think slowly about what happened; in a way, they're pictures of my mind.

This book is about my family's experience of the war – as far as I know it. I hope it will encourage you to look into your own family history, no matter where you come from. Because, chances are, you will arrive at your relatives' migration from somewhere or other to where you live now.

And along the way, you will uncover awful and amazing stories. Stories which deserve to be remembered.

For me, this is still an unfolding story: there are questions I can't yet answer. Maybe one day, I'll know everything...

But here's the story so far, right from the beginning.

Me aged ten, in Pinner

1

I grew up in a peaceful sort of a place called Pinner, to the north of London – full of people who caught the train to the centre of town in the morning and only came back in the evening.

My family lived in a flat over a shop: me, my mother Connie, my father Harold and my brother Brian. In the evenings, I played in a stony alleyway at the back of the shop, and every day I walked across the Memorial Park to school with my friend "Harrybo". (His real name was Brian Harrison, but we all called him that.) He and I used to talk about wild animals, insects, the books we had read – and radios. He was mad keen on old radios: he liked to take them apart and put them back together.

Sometimes grown-ups talked about "The War", and they always meant the Second World War. At the time, it seemed to me that The War only existed in the stories they told. I knew a bomb had landed in a park near where we lived.

One bomb. That was it.

But quite a few of our dads had been in the army. My dad was American, so he had been in the United States Army. He still had some of his uniform and kit: a cooking pan, a special kind of spade called an "entrenching tool" and little brass badges saying **US ARMY**. I loved listening to his stories about his time as a soldier and I loved the way he put on an American accent when he told them.

Dad wasn't ever in a battle. He was sent out to Berlin and told to write reports on the army's time there, so he went round the different bases to find out what was going on. One colonel thought that my dad had come to spy on him – to see if he was doing anything he shouldn't have been.

"Do you like mushrooms?" asked the colonel.

"I do and I don't," said Dad.

"I can give you as many as you want," came

the reply, and he took my dad down into the old bomb shelters under the streets ... where he had built a mushroom farm. He was using the mushrooms as a bribe, so that Dad wouldn't put anything about it in his report.

"Thousands of mushrooms!" Dad would say. "Right there, in the middle of a bombed-out city. People were starving, living in cellars, under the rubble – and he was growing mushrooms!"

I would imagine that.

Another time, a friend of my dad's wanted to know what had happened to a colleague who had worked in the Berlin Natural History Museum. It was midwinter, deep snow everywhere, but my dad still set out to find the museum. As he drew nearer to where it should have been, he could see ruined bits of building sticking up out of the snow – and in between the broken towers, there was the skeleton of a giant dinosaur.

I would imagine that too.

There was nothing like that round our way. Though one day, a boy came to school and said that he had found an old bomb shelter in the Memorial Park. So when it was getting dark, my friends and I went and levered off the metal cover, then climbed down the ladder into the shelter.

There were beds still with blankets on them and bits of rubbish on the floor. We got scared standing there in the dark and climbed out – but I think maybe we didn't put the metal cover back properly because, not long afterwards, the park wardens put earth over the top of it.

I started to wonder who had been down there and what it had really been like in Pinner during The War.

There were dinosaur skeletons
standing there in the middle of nowhere.
Great bones and skulls
rising up out of the snow
amongst heaps of broken brick
and broken glass.

"I'll never forget the sight
of those dinosaur skeletons,"
my dad said.

I've never forgotten them either –
though I never saw them.

From **Skeletons**

2

At the weekends we'd sometimes go and see our relatives. To visit Mum's family we used to ride on the Metropolitan line in train carriages that had little doors with brass handles.

On the handles it said *Live in MetroLand* in beautiful curly writing. MetroLand was just another name for the area around the Metropolitan line, but I thought it was its own country – separate from London, from England, from The War. I felt proud to live there and memorized the names of stations all the way up to Baker Street, where we had to get off.

From Baker Street, we would catch the bus to Hackney where Mum's parents (my grandparents) and her brother Ronnie lived in a ground-floor flat. We called my grandparents "Bubbe" and "Zeyde", which means "Granny" and "Granddad" in Yiddish.

Uncle Ronnie was studying physics – he

used to help my brother Brian with his science homework. Zeyde worked in a factory that made boys' school caps. And Bubbe kept chickens in the yard out the back. She took me to the market to buy bagels and all sorts of other food we didn't eat in Pinner, like chopped herring, chopped liver and a kind of yogurt called "smatana".

When we ate the bagels, Zeyde always said, "Save the hole for me." And once we had finished eating, he would always fall asleep and snore. Later, when he woke up, he'd say, "Did I snore?" and everyone would say, "No!"

Zeyde used to take me to a big park called Hackney Downs. That was where he liked to hang around with his friends, who all spoke in Yiddish. They told lots of jokes and every time I was there they would say to Zeyde, "Is this your grandson, Frank?" – in English, but with a very strong accent.

"Yes," he'd say.

"Nice-looking boy," they'd reply. Always that. And then they would all laugh.

When we came back from the park we played games. First we would play draughts ... and Zeyde always won. Next we would play chess ... and Zeyde always won. And then we would play fox and chickens, and guess what? Zeyde always won!

After that, I would ask him to show me the ship in the bottle on the mantelpiece – and wonder how the ship got inside the glass. "Ah-hah!" Zeyde would say ... and then put it back.

All of a sudden, it would be time to leave. Zeyde would give me and my brother half-a-crown each – though Mum would tell him he shouldn't.

And on the way home, I used to think about the ship sailing along the mantelpiece when we weren't there.

Bagel

On Sundays,

we go over to see Bubbe and Zeyde.

Bubbe takes me to the bagel shop to buy bagels.

There are hundreds and hundreds of them.

Then we take them home.

We sit down to eat the bagels,

and Zeyde says,

"Save the hole for me."

So I eat a bit of the bagel.

Then I say,

"Do you want the hole now, Zeyde?"

And he says, "No, there's too much bagel

round the hole.

I just want the hole."

So I eat some more bagel.

And I say,

"Do you want the hole now, Zeyde?"

And he says, "No, there's too much bagel.

I just want the hole."

So I eat some more

until all that's left is a tiny, tiny little

ring of bagel

round the hole.

And I say, "Do you want the hole now, Zeyde?"

And he says, "No, I can still see some

bagel round the hole."

So then I eat the tiny, tiny ring of bagel

round the hole

and there is no bagel left.

And Zeyde looks at me, and says,

"So? You couldn't save me the hole?"

3

My other grandma, my dad's mother, lived in East London with my Aunt Sylvia and her husband. Her name was Rose, but my dad called her "Ma" and we called her "Grandma". She was ill by the time we knew her, so she just used to sit there in her chair, watching us all.

Grandma had been born in England, but her parents came from Poland. And while she was living in London, she had met and married a Polish man called Morris - my grandfather. They had two children before moving to Massachusetts in the USA, where they had three more children.

Then Grandma and Morris split up, and Grandma came back to London with their three youngest children: my dad Harold, Aunt Sylvia and their brother Wallace, who sadly died not long after they arrived. Morris and the two eldest children, Sidney and Laurie, stayed in America.

Sometimes, when we sat round the kitchen

table, Brian and I would ask Dad about his family. He told us that, after he came to England, he didn't ever see his dad Morris again – which seemed to make him very sad.

He told us Morris had a brother, Max (Dad's uncle, so, my great-uncle). Like Morris, Max migrated from Poland and ended up in America. He got married and had three children: Ted, Olga and William. Dad hadn't ever met them.

But Dad's father Morris and his uncle Max had six other brothers and sisters. Three sisters and a brother who had stayed in Poland, where their parents, Jonas and Marta, were from originally. They were Stella, Bella, Genia and Willi. Then there were two more brothers who had migrated to France, called Oscar and Martin.

"One of them was a clock-mender," Dad said, "and the other one was a dentist."

"What happened to them all – the brothers

and sisters in Poland and France?" I asked.

Dad shrugged. "I don't know," he said. "They were there at the beginning of the war, but they had gone by the end. I suppose they died in the camps."

In the camps? I thought. *What camps?*

It made me think of school holidays: we used to go camping and it nearly always rained...

But Dad didn't mean camps like that.

Sometimes, on TV, they used to show what concentration camps were like. They said that hundreds of thousands, probably millions, of people were killed in these camps.

I would lie in bed and think about this. It seemed horrifying. Awful. But I didn't really get it.

Why did they put my great-aunts and great-uncles in these camps? And why did they kill them?

And now they were gone. No way of finding out anything at all about them. They had just disappeared – we didn't even have any pictures of them.

All that was left was my dad's shrug.

The Absentees

There are gaps,
there are blanks,
in the house
of my life;
there's a face,
nothing more,
something gone
from my life.

She was here,
he was there,
in the rooms
of my life;
there's a place
for them both
in the words
of my life.

Written for Holocaust Memorial Day, 2018

4

The language my Bubbe and Zeyde spoke –
Yiddish – was Jewish. The food they ate – bagels,
chopped herring, chopped liver, smatana – was
Jewish. Their friends were all Jewish, too.

As far as I know, they weren't religious: they
didn't go to synagogue to worship. But they still
kept up lots of Jewish traditions, which had
been passed on to them by their parents and
grandparents and great-grandparents.

You might be wondering why that matters.
Well, it matters because, in the 1920s, the
economy crashed all around the world. Germany
was hit hard: people were miserable and they
wanted someone to blame.

And, around the same time, Adolf Hitler
wrote the book *Mein Kampf* ("My Struggle"), in
which he said all of Germany's problems were
because of "the Jews". More than that, Hitler and
the party he led, the Nazis, said "the Jews" were
an inferior race – lesser than "pure" Germans,

who he called "Aryans".

Even more than that, the Nazis said that not only were Jewish companies driving Germans out of business, but Jewish culture was replacing German culture and traditions.

This is called scapegoating: blaming a person or group of people for something bad that's happened. And when I hear racists in action today, when I hear people saying racist things while pretending that they are being "realistic", I go back to Hitler's speeches where he explained "realistically" that the problem for Germans was the Jews.

The Nazis' racism worked. Once they were in power, they gradually put into place all sorts of laws that targeted Jewish people. This was part of the Nazis' "antisemitism" - a racism that is directed at Jews.

There were laws to stop Jewish people from going to university. Laws to stop Jewish people from appearing in public life: as politicians, as entertainers, as doctors.

Eventually there were laws that prevented Jewish people from having jobs and owning property. And then later, during The War, there were laws to take Jewish people from their homes and force them to live in open-air prisons, which some people called "ghettos".

This was all leading towards what the Nazis called the "Final Solution of the Jewish Question", which they hoped would be the genocide of all the Jews in Europe. "Genocide" is the killing (or attempted killing) of a whole group of people. Today, this genocide is often called "The Holocaust".

At the same time, the Nazis targeted other groups of people with a view to killing them all, including Polish people, Roma people and everyone who they thought had something "wrong" with them genetically.

The Nazis and those who helped them (known as "collaborators") rounded people up, sometimes killing them straight away, sometimes enslaving them, often working them to death on farms, in mines and in factories making guns and bombs.

They also sent them to "ghettos" and those camps I mentioned before – labour and death camps, where people died from disease or lack of food, or were gassed by "killing machines".

It's incredibly difficult to find out the names of everyone who died, because so many documents were destroyed in the last days of The War. For the same reason, it's also hard to know exactly how many people died. But we know that the Second World War was the deadliest time in human history.

And we think that about 15 million people were killed during the Holocaust. Nearly 6 million of these people were Jews.

When they do war,
they forget how to count.
They forget how to count,
and that's how they do it.

They come,
they kill;
they kill,
they go.

No numbers.
No names.
They disappear them.
They vanish them.
That's how they do it.

They come,
they kill;
they kill,
they go.

And it's
"worth it",
they say,
"it's worth it, believe us",
if you forget how to count.

If you forget the numbers.
If you forget the names.
If you forget the faces.

When they do war,
they forget how to count.
They forget how to count,
and that's how they do it.

But we're counting.
Watch us:
we're counting.
Listen.
We're counting.
And
we count.

From **Counting**

5

My mum and dad were teachers, which meant that we had long summer holidays. We camped in Wales and Yorkshire, and sometimes we went abroad. I remember holidays all over France: in Brittany in the north, the Jura Mountains in the east, the Pyrenees in the south and the Ardèche in the middle.

I loved France so much that for a while I wanted to be French! I loved the mountains and I loved the beaches. I loved the smell of herbs like thyme on the hillsides. I started to learn how to speak French, and I loved the language. I started to like French food and learn French songs. I bought French clothes and tried to look French.

When I was a teenager, I stayed for six weeks in a kids' summer camp called a "colonie de vacances". I was the only English person there and spoke only French for six weeks. We played football, table tennis and volleyball, climbed mountains and went canoeing. I learned all sorts of slang words, like "la flotte" for water, and "les godasses" for shoes. When we went canoeing we rowed through a gorge where no one lived and saw eagles flying round the rocks.

I liked studying the big insects and mini-beasts in France: the praying mantis, the flying grasshoppers, the scorpions... When I got lonely, I wrote to Mum and Dad and told them how I was getting on. I told them there was no road to the colonie: we had to cross the river on a little chariot hanging from wires. We used to dive off it into the river.

And I told them how we once went for a midnight hike and came to a special monument high up in the mountains. It marked where the Nazis had killed the men from the village during The War, and everyone went quiet when we looked at it.

I was sad to come home, so the next year I

went to France again. I travelled all over and met up with a French family who had a holiday place high up in the Pyrenees. For several summers I stayed there and helped them with the harvest – I even learned some words in the language they spoke there, which they called "patois".

Over the years, I kept going back to France, learning more French and reading lots of French books. Which is a big part of why I started to wonder about my two great-uncles, Oscar and Martin – the ones who, out of all those brothers and sisters, had ended up in France.

I wanted to know more – and not just because I could speak French, which meant I could look through French records without a translator. It was also because their stories were tied up with this country that I loved. A country that had suffered during The War.

France joined the Allies in 1939, soon after

the Nazis and the Soviet Union invaded Poland; one year later, the Nazis invaded France and, in six short weeks, seized control of Paris.

At first, they tried to behave "legally" – as they saw it, of course. They made a deal with the French government and divided the country in two: there was one part that the Nazis occupied, stationing their troops there and ruling over it, and another that was run by a new French government.

This was called the "Vichy" government, because that's where it was based, and it was meant to be independent – though it was really overseen by the German army.

But it turned out that some of the French people in power shared Nazi ideas about the Jews: they wanted to "Francify" France, like the Nazis wanted to make Germany more German.

And they wanted to do it by removing any Jewish influences.

OCCUPIED FRANCE 1940–1942

It is illegal in France to list people who are French citizens by their religion. So the Vichy officials made lists of Jews who were living in France but had been born somewhere else.

And they handed those lists over to the Nazis.

I'm not on the list

I'm not on the list.
I'm not on the list.
All I have to do
is tell them if I know someone
who should be on the list.

If I don't
tell them that I know someone
who should be on the list,
then I'll be on a list of people
who don't help them make the list.

And people in my family
will be on a list of people
in families of people
who don't help them make the list
of people who should be on the list.

If you're not on the list,
or the list of the people
who don't help them make the list,
or the list of people who know people who
don't help them make the list ...
you're OK.
It's all OK.
It's going to be all right.

6

I really wanted to find out more about Oscar and Martin, but there wasn't much to go on. So I decided to take a trip to America and visit my relatives over there.

By that time, my grandfather Morris had died and so had his brother Max. But Max's son and daughter – Ted and Olga – were alive and well.

I stayed with Ted and his wife in Manchester, Connecticut. Ted told me stories about Morris: how he used to come and stay with his family, how he drove a convertible and how he had five smart suits that he kept in a trunk.

I met Olga at a big party which Ted's children Teddy and Rachel had organized for him. (It was his birthday but the party was meant to be a surprise, so we all had to pretend we'd come to celebrate Hanukkah!)

When I asked her about her French uncles, Oscar and Martin, Olga told me she used to write to them when she was a girl.

Wow! Suddenly here was a tiny bit of information about them.

"Did they answer?" I said. "Have you got any of the letters they sent you?"

She said no. "I wrote to them to teach myself French."

Trying not to feel too disappointed, I asked, "Where did they live?"

"I think it was a place called 'Metz'," she said. "And maybe, another time, a place nearby – 'Nancy'. One of them was a clock-mender and the other was a dentist. I'm not sure which was which."

That was just what my dad had told me. "Anything else?"

She thought for a moment. "I think they lived in a street called 'Rue de Thionville'."

Now I had something: a clue.

When I got home, I looked up "Rue de Thionville" and I found that there were quite a few of them – there's a town called "Thionville" in north-eastern France and any number of roads in or out of its centre are called by the same name.

I went online and searched for "Oscar Rosen", "Martin Rosen", "Rue de Thionville", "Metz", "Nancy"... I tried all sorts of different ways of phrasing it, over months and months.

But no matter what I tried, nothing came up.

In the family they were always the French uncles.

The ones who were there before the war.

The ones who weren't there after the war.

The family said that one of them was a dentist

and the other one mended clocks. **And that was it.**

Not quite it. There was a street that the relatives

here and in America talked about, which was:

"Rue de Thionville". And places in France:

Nancy and Metz. And one of the brothers

was Oscar and the other was Martin. **And that was it.**

Though Olga, in America, nearly as small as a walnut,

said that she used to write letters to them to learn

how to write French.

And that was it.

                              But I wouldn't let it go.

From **Not Just For Them**

At the Wiener Library in 2018

7

I went down all sorts of different paths, every one of which turned out to be a dead end.

For instance, around that time I was in an airport waiting for a plane and got talking to a young French guy. He said he was from Metz, so I told him I was trying to find out things about my lost relatives and I thought one or other – or both – of them lived there before The War.

He was a student and knew how to find out about things like that, so we swapped emails.

A few weeks later, I got a message – I rushed to open it. This could be it, the big breakthrough. I scrolled through his email and ... nothing. He hadn't found a thing!

Eventually, I had to admit that I'd reached a full stop. There was just nothing – no information about Oscar and Martin. So to distract myself, I started to read more about what happened in Europe towards the end of The War.

I read how, to the Nazis' twisted minds, there were two purposes to the Holocaust: to remove people, but also to remove the memory of them. They were convinced that Jewish people had destroyed European culture, so they wanted to remove all Jewish influences from art and music and literature.

They looted and destroyed work by Jewish artists, and art collections belonging to Jewish families. They burned thousands and thousands of books they had decided were "un-German".

Before starting my research I knew The War had spanned several continents and lasted six years (1939–45). During that time many different countries were involved, incuding all the countries in what was called the British Empire.

On 6 June, Britain and America, along with troops from Canada, invaded France on what became known as D-Day. They pushed back the

German army, and the French Resistance freed Paris and other parts of France.

But now I found out that Germany ended up fighting on two fronts: the Russians were advancing from the east and the Americans, British and Canadians from the west.

When the Nazis knew they were losing, they wanted to hide what they had done. They destroyed some of the camps they had built – and they tried to destroy any evidence that the millions and millions of people they had killed ever existed.

As I read this, I felt so angry and sad that I hadn't found a way to remember Oscar and Martin. No one in my family knew anything about them, and this frustrated me beyond words. It meant the Nazis had succeeded. And the last thing I wanted was for them to have won.

So now I really, really wanted to know more. *They can't get away with this*, I said to myself.

Names

When we talk about sisters and brothers

and fathers and mothers

and we get to the sisters and brothers of my father's father

my dad shuts his eyes and says he'd rather not talk about that.

But we ask for their names

and where they are

where do they live and is it far?

And bit by bit he tells us their names

and that none of them are alive

there was a war, he explains.

And we sit and we think about us sitting here

how sisters and brothers could just disappear

but because Mum and Dad were in a different place

they could stay here where they were safe

my mother and father were able to survive

and here we are now and we're all alive.

8

One day, entirely out of the blue, an email arrived from America.

It was from Teddy – the son of Max's son, Ted, who I had stayed with in Connecticut. And Teddy had news. Not any old news: big news.

When he was a little boy, Ted had split up with Teddy's mother. Her brother – Teddy's uncle – had just died and among his papers were four letters. Do you know who they were from?

Amazingly and incredibly, two of them were from Oscar!

Teddy sent the letters to me as email attachments and I pored over them.

The first thing I noticed was Oscar's address: *11 Rue Mellaise, Niort*. Niort? That's on the other side of France from Metz, where everyone said that he and Martin lived! It's more than four hundred miles away, far over to the west.

The letters are all written to Max – Oscar's brother.

Here are Oscar's letters:

CARTE POSTA[LE]

Exp.
Rosen,11 rue Mellaise
NIORT (Deux Sévres)
France

Sonst kein Neues,als ich
Euch herzlich grüsse und
küsse,Euer denkender Oscar.
Von meiner 1.Frau folgen an
Euch viele Grüsse

Monsieur

Max Rosen

96,West Cedar St.

Boston

U. S. A.   Mass

Niort le 18-3-1940.

Meine Lieben.

Euren L.Brief v.17-1-1940, habe ich erhalten,es freut
mich dass Ihr gesund seid und das Gleiche kann ich Euch
mitteilen. Auch hoffe ich dass Ihr mein Schreiben V.6/2
erhalten habet. Nur wundert mich sehr dass Ihr an mich
so wenig schreibt. So wie kann ich Euch mitteilen, dass
ich aus Polen noch immer kein Lebenszichen erhalten habe. Jetzt frage ich Euch an ob Ihr schon ein Schreiben
aus Polen bekommen habet,falls ja, so bitte mir eine
Copie (nicht das Original) einzusenden. Ich bitte Euch
nochmals und gibt mir sofort Bescheid.

Was anbelangt mein Geschäft,kann ich Euch mitteilen,
dass ich schon seit den 20/8-1939, nicht schaffe und dass
wir von den Ersparnissen leben. Es wird täglich in der C[a]
Cassa weniger.

Deinen L.Brief habe ich an Martin eingeschickt.

Es freut mich dass Du 1.Bruder nach Polen Geld schickst
leider kann ich dasselbe nicht tun.

Rosen
96 West Cedar St.
Boston, Mas[s]

Rosen, 11 Rue Mellaise
Niort (Deux Sévres)
France
18 March, 1940

To:
Monsieur Max Rosen
96, West Cedar St.
Boston Mass U.S.A.

My dears,

 I have received your dear letter dated 17 January, 1940. I am glad that you are healthy and I can tell you the same about us. I also hope that you received my letter dated 6 February, 1940. But I am very surprised that you write to me so little. I can inform that I have still not received a sign of life from Poland. Now I am asking you whether you have already received a letter from Poland. If yes, please send me a copy (not the original).

I am asking you again and let me know immediately.

As for my business, I can tell you that since 20 August, 1939, I have not worked and that we live from our savings. Our money is getting less every day.

I forwarded your dear letter to Martin.

I am glad that you are sending money to our dear brother.

I am pleased to hear that you, dear brother, send money to Poland.

Unfortunately I cannot do the same.

Otherwise no news. I am sending you heartfelt greetings and kisses.

Your Oscar who is thinking of you. My dear wife sends many regards.

Oscar can't earn any money because, along with millions of other French people, he's fled from eastern France to western France. He and his wife are surviving on whatever savings they had.

They must have been very scared for the future. But more than anything else, Oscar sounds desperate to find out what's happened to his brother and three sisters in Poland – he must have had a sense that the situation was even worse over there.

Here's his second letter:

My dears,

Only today did I receive your dear letter dated 29 February. I hope that you already received my card dated 18 March. We are glad to hear that you are in good health and I can tell you the same from us. We were very pleased to receive your letter and we thank you very much.

I just learned from you that dear Bella is no more in Biala. I tried to make enquiries, but unfortunately I can't get any information.

I am very surprised that you have not yet received any news from Poland. You live in a neutral country, therefore it is much easier for you to find out something about our sisters in Poland. Who knows whether they are still alive.

Write immediately. Also let me know right away whether you received this card. You may also write to me in Yiddish. I learned that it is best to write in Polish to Poland, and up to 25 words, not more. If you receive a letter from Poland, *only* send me a *copy*.

Nothing else new, as I am awaiting good news.

Best regards, your brother, brother-in-law,

Oscar

My dear wife also sends you many regards and wishes you the best. Awaiting immediate answers, as it takes very long.

That's not all - Teddy had found another two letters from Oscar's sister Stella and her husband, Bernard. They had been living in west Poland with their son Michael at the beginning of The War.

Michael was just seventeen when Poland was invaded - by the Nazis to the west and the Soviets to the east.

This was because of a shaky, short-lived alliance between Nazi Germany and the Soviet Union - who both wanted to claim Poland as their own.

Stella and Bernard were desperate to do something for Michael - and both of the letters to Max beg him to "take my only child".

Here's the first one from Stella:

From:
Rechnitz
Dombrowa 6/S
Schlesischestr. 14
22 January, 1941

To:
Mr Max Rosen
West Cedar 96
Boston Mass U.S.A.

Dear Brother,
I have written to you several times and urged you fervently to take in my only child, Micha Rechnitz in Joszkar – 6 Ta, Maryjskoja A.S.S.R. pocstowy Jasscryk No. 8 barack / 7. Soviet Union.
He was sent away from Lemberg and only America can rescue him. Therefore I am

fervently asking you to take the necessary steps immediately. Many thousands have already gone to America. I am asking you again to fulfil my request. I have sent you my son's birth certificate. Born 16 November, 1923 in Dombrowa 6/S.

What are you doing, my dears? Kisses to you and your dear wife. Maybe for now you can send him a few dollars? I beg you very much.

Thousands of Jewish people tried to make their way to America, just as Stella says. But while some succeeded, many more were turned away – as they were by governments all over Europe.

One of the most famous examples is from 1939, when a ship called the *St. Louis* set sail from Nazi Germany carrying more than 900 Jewish refugees. The ship made it all the way to Cuba, a trip of some four thousand miles ... only for the US government to send it and its passengers all the way back to Europe.

Here is the next letter from Stella:

11 February, 1941

Dear Brother,

I hope you have already taken the steps to take in my son. Maybe you could adopt him to make this work?

Dear brother, I urge you. For now send him a few dollars and packages with food because he has nothing. I fervently urge you to send something as soon as possible. Don't be upset with me but only you ... [remainder of the sentence obscured by airmail stamp]

Kisses to you and to your dear wife and children.

Your sister
Stella

Stella is frantic to do something for her only son: a seventeen-year-old Jewish boy, whose world is falling apart all around him, and who will surely die if he stays with his family in west Poland.

But did the letters work? What happened to Micha (Michael)?

This part of the puzzle, I knew already.

Not long after the end of The War, there was a knock on my Aunt Sylvia's door in London. A young man was standing on her doorstep.

"Lady Sylvia?" he asked.

She let him in – and, bit by bit, it became clear that the young man was Michael!

We don't know whether Max tried and failed to get him to America, but, in the end, Stella and Bernard put Michael on an eastbound train to get him away from the Nazis.

When Michael arrived in the Soviet half of Poland, he was sent to a prison camp in Russia. But then, in 1941, the Nazis decided they wanted to control *all* of Poland, not just the west – so they fought their way east and their alliance with the Soviets crumbled to bits.

Michael was offered the chance to join a new Polish Free Army, fighting on the side of the Soviets – who had gone over to the Allies' side. And he accepted. He travelled thousands of miles with them, fighting battle after battle, all the way to Italy.

When The War was over, Michael didn't want to go back to Poland. Everyone knew, by then, that all the Jews had gone from Poland. Nearly all of them killed. So he thought he would try to get to America to find his relatives there: his uncles Morris and Max.

In the end he only got as far as London, where he stayed with Sylvia. He went on to become a taxi driver, got married and had children of his own.

Michael never saw his parents Stella and

SOVIET
UNION

Soviet Union
occupied
Poland on
17 September,
1939

Lemberg

POLAND

EAST
PRUSSIA

CZECHOSLOVAKIA

Soviet Union

Germany

GERMANY

Germany invaded
Poland 1 September,
1939

Bernard again. He never found out what happened to them. All he had was one photo of his mother ... and now, these letters.

But it was because of their actions that he survived.

On the Move Again

You know
You gotta go.
No time to grieve.
You just gotta leave.
Get away from the pain.
On the move again.

Take the train.
Catch a plane.

Make the trip
In a ship.

Take a hike.
Ride a bike.

Go by car.
Going far.

Use your feet
On the street.

Get stuck
In a truck.

Then you arrive
And you're alive.

You arrive.
You're alive.

What you leave behind
Won't leave your mind.

But home is where you find it.
Home is where you find it.
Home is where you find it.
Home is where you find it.

9

I went back to the two letters from Oscar and looked at the address he had sent them from ... and then, straight away, I searched for *11 Rue Mellaise, Niort* online.

I used Google Street View and – incredibly! – the house is still standing. But why had Oscar and his wife been living there?

I looked up what had been happening in France in 1940, the year Oscar wrote to Max. I found out that when France was invaded by the German army, who came marching in from the east, millions of people fled to the west and the south of the country.

In France it's called "L'exode" or "The Exodus", which is the name in the Bible given to the time when the Jews fled from Egypt.

Now I knew why Oscar had left eastern France: to get away from the Nazis. But I wanted to know what happened to the Jewish people in Niort. Was there any way of finding out?

Again, I searched online and found the title of a book called *Les Chemins de la Honte: Itinéraire d'une Persécution*, by a man called Jean-Marie Pouplain. The title means: "Paths of Shame: The Road to a Persecution".

I ordered it and waited ages for it to arrive – so long that I was sure it had got lost in the post. But it did appear eventually, just as my family and I were packing up all our things.

We were leaving a house I had lived in for 25 years. Surrounded by big boxes, I ripped open the package and turned straight to the index. There I saw that the name "Rosen" was mentioned on fourteen different pages.

The first time was on page 34. I quickly flipped to there – even as the removal lorry pulled into our drive – and in a list of names which I could see were Jewish, it said in French:

Rosen, Jeschie, né le 23 juin, 1895, polonais,

bonneterie, marié à Kesler, Rachel, née en
1910, 11 Rue Mellaise.

This means:

Rosen, Jeschie, born 23 June, 1895, Polish,
sock and stocking seller, married to Kesler,
Rachel, born in 1910, 11 Rue Mellaise.

It was the right address and the age fitted. So even though it was "Jeschie" Rosen and not Oscar Rosen, surely this was my father's uncle?

I looked up "Jeschie" and found that it's often a nickname taken from the Hebrew name "Yehoshua". Jews who belong to a synagogue are given a special Jewish name as well as their official one, so I wondered if maybe Oscar's Jewish name had been "Yehoshua" and people liked to call him "Jeschie".

It was just a guess, but it felt right.

I went through the rest of the book, while my family waited impatiently for me to get into the car. It really was time for us to move to our new house! But I just couldn't tear myself away.

On one of the pages, it said that Jeschie Rosen was an "horloger de carillon" – a "mender of chiming clocks". That fitted the family story, that one of the brothers was a clock-mender... But it seemed that Jeschie had been forced to make a living selling socks and stockings, even though he was trained in mending clocks.

I read that the local official – the "Prefect" or "Sub-Prefect" – had drawn up lists of Jewish people. They were forced to wear a yellow star labelled "Juif" ("Jew") and had to put up a sign saying "Entreprise Juive" ("Jewish business") where they worked.

I was horrified. I knew about the yellow stars, and I'd thought about what it must have been like, to be marked out by the government as some kind of inferior being. But I didn't know about the "Jewish business" label and I couldn't believe how dangerous that was. They would have been a target for anyone who wanted to attack them for being Jewish.

On another page in the book I found the word "forain" next to Jeschie's name, which usually means someone selling things in a market: I pictured him with that sign on his market-stall and that badge on his jacket.

Perhaps even worse, the book said that at the time everything Jews owned – every bit of it – was "Aryanized".

That word ... *Aryanized*. It means something horrible. It means that everything Jeschie and his wife Rachel owned stopped being "Jewish" and was made "Aryan". It means that all of their belongings were taken away and given to the government in Vichy France.

Now I was disgusted. But what had actually

happened to Oscar-Jeschie? I still didn't know.

I noticed that the rest of the people on the list with Oscar were shipped from Niort to a place near Paris called Drancy ... and then to Auschwitz, a place where most of them had been killed.

I had another book called *The Deportation of the Jews from France* and I had often looked in it trying to find Martin and Oscar. There were several different Martin and Oscar Rosens, but I had no way of knowing if any of them could have been my father's uncles.

But this time I was looking up a much less common name: "Jeschie". And, sure enough, there he was – in a list of people who were all part of the same convoy.

This is what the book said:

Convoy 62, a convoy of 1,200 Jews leaving Paris-Bobigny at 11.50 a.m. on 20 November

1943. Arrived Auschwitz, 25 November, as
cabled by SS Colonel Liebehenschel. 1181
arrived. There had been 19 escapees, they
were young people, who escaped at 8.30 p.m.
near Lerouville. In the convoy there were 83
children who were less than twelve years old.
Out of the convoy 241 were selected for work
and given numbers 164427–164667. Women
numbered 69036–69080 were selected too.
914 were gassed straightaway. In 1945, there
were 29 survivors, 27 men and 2 women.

Here was the horrific reason why my dad,
all those years earlier, had shrugged and said,
"They were there at the beginning of the war but
they had gone by the end."

I stared at the word "convoy". It meant a train
of cattle-trucks with all of those people – men,
women and children – squeezed inside. Pulling
out of a station in Paris and taking five days to

travel through France, across Germany and into Poland: a journey of 1,500 km.

I searched online for more information about Convoy 62 and eventually found a memoir written by a man called Henry Bily – one of the other prisoners on board. Here is his description of the awful journey:

[T]he children cried endlessly. They were hungry, they were afraid and they were tired. They had never been through such a nightmare, or experienced such a stench. Or such a noise! How many hours had passed? Already, half of the people in our truck seemed completely listless. Of the other half, how many were even lucid? As for me, after finishing the bread that I was given at the beginning of our journey, I was beginning to feel very hungry...

Each of us tried to guess where we were. Each
of us tried to imagine our final destination.
What would be our fate? It would be useless to
recall everything that took place during that
terrible journey. The spread of misinformation
and lies, the smell of the lavatory bucket in
the middle of the truck, and the unbearable
overcrowding, made us no longer quite
human.

— Translated from *Destin a Part: Seul déporté*
rescapé de la rafle de Clans du 25 Octobre 1943
by Henry Bily

As I read these words, I wondered about the
"young people" who had managed to escape. I
wondered how they did that; perhaps forcing the
door open and jumping out?

And I thought about the people who hadn't
managed to escape. Who had arrived at this

horrific destination, Auschwitz ... a huge place, which was in different parts a camp, a factory, a forced labour prison and an "extermination" centre.

I thought of the films I had seen of people being separated, lined up and marched off in different directions. The awful huts with people dying of starvation and disease. The gas chambers and crematoria – killing people by gassing them and then burning their bodies.

I was overwhelmed by the idea that it could have happened to my father's uncle, his wife and probably his brother.

They had spent long, happy years living in eastern France, only to be driven from their home and killed, one way or another, in this awful place.

There was something else: in this book, it said that Jeschie was born in "Oświęcim".

Do you know what that means? "Oświęcim" is

the Polish word for "Auschwitz".

The terrible truth is that Jeschie was born in the same town where the Nazis built their camp.

I wondered when it was he realized that the death camp he was going to was so near his home.

People run away from war.

Sometimes we get away.

Sometimes we don't.

Sometimes we're helped.

Sometimes we aren't.

From **People Run**

10

I thought perhaps now I had all the information I would ever have about my missing relatives. But I went on searching online.

One day, up popped the names of Oscar and his wife Rachel – on a monument and in some papers from a French town called Sedan.

There was even a picture of the monument, showing an engraved list of the names of people who were "victims of Nazi barbarism".

Why were they on a monument in a Jewish cemetery in Sedan? No one in the family had ever mentioned Sedan – it's in northern France, close to Belgium. So who had put their names there?

The author of the papers was a man called Gerald Dardart. I wrote to him and he told me that Oscar and Rachel had lived in Sedan, but when they were picked up by the Nazis they were in Nice. That's the town in the south of France, pronounced "neece".

And Gerald Dardart said they were arrested by the Nazis in a hotel.

Once again, I needed books to find out more ... and what I found out was utterly sad.

Nice and its surrounding area wasn't occupied by the Germans during the Second World War, but by one of the other Axis powers: Italy. And it seems that while the Nazis were deporting Jews from the rest of France, the Italians were not. More than that: when the Nazis asked the Italians to hand over Jews living in Nice and nearby, they refused.

And even more than that: in Nice there lived a Jewish-Italian man called Angelo Donati, who was doing everything he could to evacuate Jewish refugees. He was working on a risky plan to save about 30,000 people. He had been trying to organize passports via his British and American contacts, and had even got hold of four ships to carry people to safety.

So how had Oscar and Rachel been captured and sent to Auschwitz?

Well, at the very moment my great-uncle arrived in Nice, the Allies were about to conquer Italy. Donati heard the news and sent a message to the American General Dwight D. Eisenhower, begging him not to announce the victory until he had got all the Jews out of Nice. He was afraid that if Eisenhower did so, the Nazis would retaliate by invading Nice and capturing Jewish people.

But I'm afraid to say that Eisenhower *did* announce the Allies' victory, and three days later, in September 1943, the Nazis marched into Nice.

And where were the Jews, including Oscar and Rachel? In hotels all over the city, waiting for Donati to get them out. Lots of them weren't even hiding: they were so sure they were going to be rescued.

They were caught. The Nazis seized them and sent them north to a camp in a housing estate called Drancy. From there they were sent to the train station Paris Bobigny...

And you know the rest.

Just another few days, and Oscar and Rachel would have escaped on the boats that Donati had ready and waiting for them.

I felt incredibly sad. They had been so close to being safe and staying alive.

Later I went to the Wiener Library in London to see if they had a list of Jewish people arrested at the Hotel Excelsior at that time. They pulled out a sheet – and on it were Oscar and Rachel Rosen.

Again, I thought about Oscar and Rachel escaping across France to Nice. A journey of nearly 1000 km. Maybe they had heard rumours: "You'll be safe in Nice!" "You'll be able to escape!" Somehow or another, they got there.

Nearly free. So nearly free. But the net had closed around them.

Dear Oscar

What did you think,
as you and Rachel
sat on the floor
of the cattle truck
as it left Paris?

Did you think of the watches
and clocks you had mended?
Did you think of the tiny springs and wheels?

You with your magnifying glass
in your eye, poring over the works
so that a Monsieur or a Madame
could tell the time,
correct to the exact second...

Did you look
through the gaps in the slats
on the side of the truck?

Did you see farmers in fields?
Women selling clothes in a market?

Did you call out?
Did you push your hands through the gaps?

Did the night come creeping in?
Did you see a light from a window
where people sat and
ate their evening meal?

Did you see in the dark
horror on Rachel's face?
Did she see horror on yours?

Did you shut her eyes?
Did she shut yours?
Thinking of children
who shut their eyes to make
the world go away?

And then
behind your eyelids
did you think of the cattle
that had once stood in the truck
as they were taken away
to the slaughterhouse?

11

With all of these new details, I had another dig about online ... and I discovered something really quite bothering.

I found a form dated February 1939 – it had been filled out by my father's cousin Olga. And it turned out she had tried to get Oscar out of France before the war, and had been asking for him to come to America.

This was both amazing and amazingly sad. Because, of course, he never went.

I asked the people who put this file on the internet if they knew whether the American authorities said that they would let Oscar in. They had no idea.

So I don't actually know whether they said yes or no. I don't know whether the US government offered him a place in America and he refused, or whether they turned him down. But, as I said before, a lot of Jews had their applications rejected. There were all sorts of papers to fill out and hoops to jump through to be accepted – and it would have taken a near-miracle for Jewish refugees to tick all of those boxes, even as their own government was stripping them of their rights as citizens.

There was something else. When Olga wrote asking for Oscar to come, she called him ... Jeschie!

Finally I had proof that people in the family called Oscar both "Oscar" and "Jeschie".

That solved that one, then – but I was left wondering why Olga and her brother Ted (my dad's cousin) had never told me she had tried to get Oscar-Jeschie to come and live with them in America.

She told me she'd written to him to improve her French, but she never told me that. Why not?

Teddy, her nephew, said it was because she felt guilty. The same reason why, mysteriously, the letters from France and Poland had been hidden away.

It was because the American brothers – my grandfather Morris and his brother Max – were ashamed. And so were Max's children, Ted and Olga.

The brothers hadn't kept in touch with the rest of their siblings during The War. At its end, when they wondered what had happened to them all – to Oscar, Martin, Bella, Stella, Genia and Willi – they had "disappeared".

The only one they knew had escaped was Stella's son, Michael. He was the one who had turned up in London after The War, with no intention of returning to Poland.

So my family clammed up and said as little as they could.

I don't blame them. Of course I don't.

It was so important to me that we found out about Oscar; that we remembered him. But I can see how it was just too much for the others. They must have felt devastated at the realization that they had lost so many members of their family. Traumatized, on their relatives' behalf.

And they must have wished that they could have done more. Or perhaps felt that they *should* have done more.

12

And that was it.

Well ... not quite!

Once again, I thought I had got to the end of my trail: found out all that I could. But a few years later, I got an email from Teddy in America. He said that his father, Ted, had died aged 103, and he had gone into his old house.

It was the place where Ted had told me about my grandfather Morris and his five suits.

Teddy said he found a cupboard that was locked. Inside were thousands of photos – and among these was a box labelled "Family Photos". He opened it up ...

... and inside were pictures of our great-uncle, Oscar! And his brother Willi and sister Stella, too, as well as their parents.

These photos had been in there the whole time when I came to the house and talked to Ted about the family.

Another of them was of my great-aunt Stella with her son, Michael. They were walking together down a street in Poland.

I quickly got in touch with Michael's son and sent it to him. He said his father was "mesmerized" by the photo. He stared and stared at it.

I hope it wasn't too much of a shock for him, to look at that photo. It was the first time he had ever seen it, and it's only the second photo he has of his mother. He took the first photo with him when he said goodbye to his parents at the beginning of the war.

The photos of Oscar show him in uniform. At first I thought it must be a French uniform, but I posted the picture on Twitter along with the information on the back of it.

Do you know what someone told me?

Oscar is wearing a uniform of the Austro-Hungarian Army – one that belonged to a regiment put together in Poland during the First World War. What's more, when I looked up the regiment, I found out that they fought in more than 35 battles alongside the German army.

Before he went to France, Jeschie Rosen had been a war hero – on the side of the Germans. A Polish man who had helped the Germans to fight a war.

I shake my head every time I think about that.

Because when it came to the Nazis deciding to get rid of the Jews, this counted for nothing.

I found these things out in order to know.

    I found these

Things out, I know now, in order to tell other

    people.

I found these things out so that Jeschie and

    Rachel will be known

But in the end I know that the point of them

    being known is

That this is a story not just for them and

    about them.

From **Not Just for Them**

13

Well, that's it.

But, still, not quite.

What about the second uncle, Martin? The other one living in France?

I couldn't help but carry on looking: searching and searching on the internet. I had wrapped up my discoveries about Oscar – and was just putting the finishing touches to this book! – when suddenly I discovered a website with a clue about what happened to Martin.

From 1943 onwards, he was living in an area of western France called the Vendée. And in 1944, the Germans sent an instruction to the French officials in the Vendée.

The police were ordered to go out and arrest the Jews in the area, in the middle of the night. That meant everyone with a Jewish connection: if someone had one Jewish and one non-Jewish parent, that person would be arrested too.

The people arrested were told to bring winter clothes, money and valuables. And the places where they had been staying should be sealed.

I wrote to a specialist library in the Vendée and asked them to send me any report that mentioned Martin Rozen or Rosen. Almost immediately they sent me back a report dated 31 January, 1944 – which told me the following.

At 2.30 in the morning, four police officers called in at a property owned by someone called Madame Bobières, in the village of Sainte-Hermine.

This property was the living quarters of "Martin Rozen".

The officers' report was full of details. They said that Martin was a jeweller – not a dentist, as I had always been told.

They said that he was 1 metre and 62 centimetres tall, with brown eyes, an oval face, a straight nose and a regular mouth.

He was dressed in yellow cotton trousers and a grey cotton jacket, wearing a Basque beret and low-heeled shoes.

He had a scar on his left cheek.

I tried to picture the scene: a little village in the countryside; four policemen in their dark blue uniforms, turning up in the middle of the night, knocking on the door of a lady's house, and then taking my great-uncle away.

Why?

The report said that Martin had been the one to answer the door that night. What did he think was going on? What did he think was going to happen to him? Was he hiding in Madame Bobières' house? Did he think he was safe in this little village, far away from the cities and the soldiers?

Had he heard about Jews being taken away and never coming back?

It made me feel desperate to read it. How

powerless Martin must have felt... Had he been angry? Or scared? Or both?

And I thought of the policemen. Didn't they think that it was terrible, to arrest someone just because they were Jewish? Somehow, they had gone back to the police station and written such detailed notes; all about what Martin looked like and what he was wearing.

What did they do then? Have breakfast? What did they say to their families? "We arrested a Jew tonight."

Or were they sorry? Sad? Guilty?

According to the report, Martin was taken to the parish hall in a town called La Roche-sur-Yon. Along with 30 other Jews arrested that night, he was put on a train to the nearby town of La Rochelle, then to a nearby city called Poitiers, then to the Drancy internment camp.

The same camp where his brother Oscar and sister-in-law Rachel had been kept, just two and a half months earlier. Though I don't think Martin could possibly have known that...

On 10 February, 1944, Martin was put on a train of cattle trucks called "Convoy 68". There were 1,500 people on that train. No one knew where the train was going – the guards wouldn't tell them. So people called their destination "Pitchipoï": a nonsense name.

But it was really headed for Auschwitz.

I found a book written by a woman called Ida Grinspan, who was on the same convoy. She was fourteen years old at the time and she describes what it was like on those trucks.

How there were families, with children. How the truck was so full, there was no room to sit down. How there was nowhere to go to the toilet. How there was a terrible smell.

When the train arrived at Auschwitz, 210 men and 61 women were selected to be killed immediately. Of the 1,500 people, 42 survived.

Martin was never seen again.

The Vendée library had sent me another piece of paper, too.

It told me that, a month and a half after Martin's arrest, his landlady Madame Bobières wrote to the officials telling them how the police had come to her house and arrested a lodger who had been staying with her for more than a year: "Mr Rosen of Jewish nationality".

"Jewish nationality"? There was no such thing! But this was the first I'd heard that Martin had been staying in this village for a year. Which made me wonder... Did everyone there know him? Had he made friends with people?

She wrote on: "A wicker basket containing some linen belonging to Mr Rosen has been left in the room, which had been sealed up by the Gendarmes." In this room, Madame Bobières wrote, "is my furniture, including a large cupboard, containing [...] sheets, clothes, linen, blankets and family papers".

So, she was writing to ask for her belongings back from Martin's room – which was still sealed.

As for Martin's belongings, Madame Bobières added, "Rosen's brother-in-law who lives in the next room, and who is French, could look after the wicker basket, which is the only piece of furniture belonging to Rosen."

Here was something – and it set my mind racing. If Martin had a "brother-in-law, who was French", that surely meant he had a French wife!

Who was she? What was her name? Was there anybody alive who knew anything about her?

There are one or two "loose ends", aren't there?

I was really surprised when the report said that Martin was a jeweller. The family story had always been that he was a dentist! I'd like to know more, but haven't found anything else yet.

You might also be wondering why Martin's surname comes out as both "Rozen" and "Rosen"; I think it's just because when people went from country to country, like Martin, they sometimes changed the way they spelt their names.

And, of course, there's the matter of this "brother-in-law" – and so, I assume, of his wife. Will I ever find out about them?

I don't know. But at least I have found out all this.

Oscar and Martin's names are engraved on the commemorative wall at the Museum of the Shoah, in Paris.

Which means that they won't be forgotten. The Nazis may have succeeded in killing them, but they can't kill their memory.

And now I've told you about them. So, as the French would say, "Souviens-toi."

Remember.

Martin Rozen (1890–1944)

My Father's Uncle

On January 31, 1944,
at 2.30 in the morning
in a village in France
four policemen knock on the door
of a woman
who has several lodgers in her house.

They take away one of them,
a man
who has done nothing wrong.

They take him to a nearby town
to put him with 30 others
who have done nothing wrong.

He is taken away with them

and put on a train

to where he and they are put

with hundreds of others

who have done nothing wrong.

He is then taken away by a train

carrying more than a thousand people

to another country

where he is put with thousands

and thousands of others

who have done nothing wrong.

And killed.

14

One of my great-uncles was a clock-mender and another was a jeweller. That's all they did wrong – which is to say, they did nothing wrong. And yet, they died for being who they were.

When we talk about the Holocaust, people often say, "Never again." That what happened to my great-uncles, and the millions of other people systematically killed by the Nazis, must never ever happen again. But we have to ask ourselves: how many attempts at genocide have there been since? The answer is quite a few.

Many more people have been through what Michael, Olga and Ted went through: losing people they loved. And of course, many more people have been through what my great-aunts and great-uncles went through: knowing that you are being killed, for no other reason than you are who you are.

Some people think that the Holocaust was intended right from the start. Others think that it came about as a result of Nazi Germany invading other countries – Poland in particular. And that this turned the Nazis from persecution and murder to genocide.

When you really look at the history of it all, you can see that these terrible things happened bit by bit: in stages.

What was going on in Germany in, say, the 1920s is not the same as what was happening in 1944, when the mass killings were taking place. So now people look for signs of what might be a dangerous slippery slope.

We have words like "racism", "prejudice", "antisemitism", "xenophobia", "discrimination" and "supremacism" to describe these first steps; they all mean slightly different things.

I'm very concerned about the prejudice I see today – all the more so because of what happened to my family. It's not that I think it's going to happen again tomorrow; it's that, if I'd been alive in 1940, it would have happened to me.

With every passing year, the number of Holocaust survivors gets smaller. We need to keep the memory of them alive: the people who died and those who survived. That's partly why I wrote this book.

But it's not the only reason. Because I'm not just concerned about antisemitism, but by all the ways in which groups of people become targets of hatred.

Especially when there's a government involved, feeding those feelings or even starting to "legally" discriminate against people. Dividing people up by religion or race. Splitting up families.

And turning away people with nowhere else to go – like the millions of refugees forced to leave their homes in Syria in recent years. Forced to travel on foot, in trucks, on boats, for thousands of miles. Men, women and children.

People like me or you.

Clock-menders and jewellers.

I want to end this book with a poem of mine that I'm very fond of.

I wrote it after looking at photos of Jews who had been imprisoned in a "ghetto" in Poland. One of them showed a couple smiling and staring up at a tree.

It felt unbearable to know (while they didn't) that they were going to die. But these people were full of joy...

I wanted to express this in a poem. I thought of despair and hope – hope and despair.

Which way round should they go? I wondered.

I knew the answer. We can't live on despair: we always have to find reason for hope. Because the world doesn't have to be this way.

More than that, we can't let it.

So, turn the page for "Today; One Day".

Today; One Day

Today

The rain has died

My shoes have died

The sun has died

My coat has died

The Earth has died

Today.

One day

The rain will flower

My shoes will laugh

The sun will sing

My coat will fly

The Earth will dance

One day.

My Family Tree

Jonas = Marta

France

Poland

Oscar = Rachel (Jeschie) Martin   Willi   Genia   Bella   Bernard = Stella

Michael

(Left) **Rachel and Oscar**

(Right) **Michael, Stella and Bella**

(Left) **Martin**

USA

England

Max = Sarah

Morris = Rose

Frank = Annie
(Zeyde) (Bubbe)

Sidney   Laurie   Sylvia   Wallace

Ronnie

Ted = Dorothy   Olga

Harold = Connie
(Dad)   (Mum)

Teddy

Michael   Brian
(me)

——— My Family   ------ My Missing Relatives in WWII

Rose and Morris

BIBLIOGRAPHY

First-hand accounts of World War II and the Holocaust

- **The Diary of a Young Girl (Definitive Edition)**
  Written by Anne Frank, edited by Otto H. Frank and Mirjam Pressler, translated by Mirjam Pressler and illustrated by Harry Brockway. Puffin Books (1997), 8+

- **A Bag of Marbles**
  Written by Joseph Joffo and translated by Martin Sokolinsky. University of Chicago Press (2001), 8+

- **In My Hands: Memories of a Holocaust Rescuer**
  Written by Irene Gat Opdyke with Jennifer Armstrong. Corgi Children's (2009), 8+

- **Behind the Secret Window: A Memoir of a Hidden Childhood During World War II**
  Written by Nellie S. Toll. Puffin Books (1993), 8+

- **The Hidden Children**
  Written by Howard Greenfeld. Houghton Mifflin Harcourt (1993), 10+

- **The Day the Nazis Came: The Astonishing True Story of a Childhood Journey from the Occupied**

Channel Islands to the Dark Heart of a German Prison Camp
Written by Stephen Matthews. John Blake Publishing (2016)

Children's non-fiction about World War II and the Holocaust

- **What Was the Holocaust? (What Was...? series)**
  Written by Gail Herman and Who HQ, illustrated by Jerry Hoare. Penguin Random House (2018), 8+
- **Hana's Suitcase: The Quest to Solve a Holocaust Mystery**
  Written by Karen Levine. Crown Books for Young Readers (2016), 8+
- **We Will Not Be Silent: The White Rose Student Resistance Movement That Defied Adolf Hitler**
  Written by Russell Freedman. Clarion Books (2016), 8+
- **The Children of Willesden Lane: A True Story of**

Hope and Survival During World War II
Written by Mona Golabek and Lee Cohen, adapted
by Emil Sher. Little, Brown Books for Young
Readers (2017), 8+

- **Beyond Courage: The Untold Story of Jewish
Resistance During the Holocaust**
Written by Doreen Rappaport. Walker Books
(2013), 12+

- **The Usborne Introduction to the Second World
War (Internet-linked)**
Written by Paul Dowswell. Usborne Publishing
(2005), 8+

- **A History of the Holocaust (Revised Edition)**
Written by Yehuda Bauer. Children's Press (1982,
updated 2001), 12+

For further information on World War II and the Holocaust online

- The Holocaust Educational Trust – het.org.uk

- The Wiener Holocaust Library – wienerlibrary.co.uk
- The Holocaust Explained, managed by The Wiener Holocaust Library – theholocaustexplained.org
- Holocaust Memorial Day Trust – HMD.org.uk
- The Anne Frank Trust UK – annefrank.org.uk
- Mémorial de la Shoah (The Shoah Memorial) – www.memorialdelashoah.org/en
- "The Holocaust Year by Year" managed by BBC iWonder – bbc.com/timelines/z86nfg8

Children's fiction about World War II and the Holocaust

- **Once**

  Written by Morris Gleitzman. Puffin Books (2006), 9+
- **The Dollmaker of Krakow**

  Written by R.M. Romero. Walker Books (2017), 9+
- **Odette's Secrets**

  Written by Maryann Macdonald. Bloomsbury (2013), 9+

- **When Hitler Stole Pink Rabbit**

  Written and illustrated by Judith Kerr.
  HarperCollins (1971), 9+

- **Hitler's Canary**

  Written by Sandi Toksvig. Yearling (2006), 9+

- **The Other Side of Truth**

  Written by Beverley Naidoo. Puffin Books (2007), 9+

- **What the Night Sings**

  Written and illustrated by Vesper Stamper. Knopf
  Books for Young Readers (2018), 12+

- **Mapping the Bones**

  Written by Jane Yolen. Penguin Books (2018), 12+

- **Anna and the Swallow Man**

  Written by Gavriel Savit. Penguin Books (2017), 12+

- **The Berlin Boxing Club**

  Written by Robert Sharenow. HarperCollins (2011),
  12+

- **Salt to the Sea**

  Written by Ruta Sepetys. Penguin Books (2016),
  12+

Children's non-fiction about refugees and displacement

- **Where Will I Live?**
  Written by Rosemary McCarney with photography by the United Nations High Commissioner for Refugees. Second Story Press (2017), 4+

- **Who Are Refugees and Migrants? What Makes People Leave Their Homes? And Other Big Questions**
  Written by Michael Rosen and Annemarie Young. Wayland (2017), 7+

- **Refugees and Migrants (Children in Our World)**
  Written by Ceri Roberts and illustrated by Hanane Kai. Wayland (2016), 6+

- **Gervelie's Journey: A Refugee Diary**
  Written by Anthony Robinson and Annemarie Young, illustrated by June Allan. Frances Lincoln Children's Books (2009), 8+

- **Hamzat's Journey: A Refugee Diary**
  Written by Anthony Robinson, illustrated by June Allan. Frances Lincoln Children's Books (2009), 8+

- **Meltem's Journey: A Refugee Diary**
  Written by Anthony Robinson, illustrated by
  June Allan. Frances Lincoln Children's Books
  (2010), 8+
- **Mohammed's Journey: A Refugee Diary**
  Written by Anthony Robinson and Annemarie
  Young, illustrated by June Allan. Frances Lincoln
  Children's Books (2011), 8+

Children's fiction about refugees and displacement

- **A Story like the Wind**
  Written by Gill Lewis and illustrated by Jo
  Weaver. Oxford University Press (2017), 8+
- **Welcome to Nowhere**
  Written by Elizabeth Laird. Macmillan Children's
  Books (2017), 9+
- **In the Sea There Are Crocodiles: The Story of
  Enaiatollah Akbari**

Written by Fabio Geda and translated by
Howard Curtis. David Fickling Books (2011), 10+

- **Refugee Boy**

  Written by Benjamin Zephaniah. Bloomsbury
  (2001), 12+

- **The Ones that Disappeared**

  Written by Zana Fraillon. Orion Children's Books
  (2017), 12+

- **The Bone Sparrow**

  Written by Zana Fraillon. Orion Children's Books
  (2016), 12+

Picture books about ...

World War II and the Holocaust

- **The Tree in the Courtyard: Looking Through
  Anne Frank's Window**

  Written by Jeff Gottesfeld and illustrated by Peter
  McCarty. Knopf Books for Young Readers (2016),
  5+

- **Benno and the Night of Broken Glass**

  Written by Meg Wiviott and illustrated by Josée Bisaillon. Kar-Ben (2010), 5+

- **I Will Come Back for You: A Family in Hiding During World War II**

  Written and illustrated by Marisabina Russo. Schwartz & Wade (2011), 6+

Refugee Experiences

- **Refuge**

  Written by Anne Booth and illustrated by Sam Usher. Nosy Crow (2015), 3+

- **The Colour of Home**

  Written by Mary Hoffman and illustrated by Karin Littlewood. Phyllis Fogelman Books (2002), 3+

- **The Day War Came**

  Written by Nicola Davies and illustrated by Rebecca Cobb. Walker Books (2018), 5+

- **My Name is Not Refugee**

  Written and illustrated by Kate Milner. The Bucket List (2017), 5+

- **The Journey**
  Written and illustrated by Francesca Sanna.
  Flying Eye Books (2016), 5+

Graphic novels about ...

World War II and the Holocaust

- **Hidden: A Child's Story of the Holocaust**
  Written by Loïc Dauvillier, and illustrated by
  Marc Lizano and Greg Salsedo. First Second
  (2014), 6+
- **Survivors of the Holocaust**
  Created by Kath Shackleton and Fettle Animation.
  Franklin Watts (2016), 9+
- **Maus, A Survivor's Tale: I, My Father Bleeds History**
  Written and illustrated by Art Spiegelman.
  Random House (1991)
- **Maus, A Survivor's Tale: II, And Here My Troubles Began**

Written and illustrated by Art Spiegelman.
Random House (1991)

Refugee Experiences

- **The Arrival**
  Written and illustrated by Shaun Tan. Hodder
  Children's Books (2007), 5+

- **Illegal: One Boy's Epic Journey of Hope and
  Survival**
  Written by Eoin Colfer and Andrew Donkin,
  illustrated by Giovanni Rigano. Hodder Children's
  Books (2017), 8+

- **Alpha: Abidjan to Gare du Nord**
  Written by Bessora, illustrated by Barroux and
  translated by Sarah Ardizzone. The Bucket List
  (2016), 11+

Audio

I have also recorded poems about my family's

experience of the Holocaust, and poems about racism and prejudice; these recordings are freely available via HistoryWorks on Audioboom: **https://audiobooks.com/playlists/4613930-michael-rosen-poems**

Films

I have presented films to accompany The Missing which you can watch or download for free via the HistoryWorks Vimeo Channel.

- **The Missing by Michael Rosen: An Illustrated Talk About My Family's Experience of the Holocaust & My Journey to Find Out What Really Happened:**
  https://vimeo.com/504195479
- **Michael Rosen reading his book The Missing, filmed for schools:**
  https://vimeo.com/501236566
- **Michael Rosen performs poetry and leads Holocaust Memorial Day:**
  https://vimeo.com/501706925

INDEX

ACKNOWLEDGMENTS

The lines of poetry on pages 4, 41 and 91 were first published in *Michael Rosen, Don't Mention the Children* (Smokestack Books, 2015); the lines on page 80 were first published in *Michael Rosen, Listening to a Pogrom on the Radio* (Smokestack Books, 2017); "Skeletons", reproduced from *QUICK, LET'S GET OUT OF HERE* written by Michael Rosen (Puffin). Copyright © Michael Rosen 1983. "Bagel", "On the Move Again" and "Today; One Day", reproduced from *MICHAEL ROSEN'S BIG BOOK OF BAD THINGS* written by Michael Rosen (Puffin). Copyright © Michael Rosen 2010. "Names" by Michael Rosen from *Jelly Boots, Smelly Boots* (Bloomsbury, 2016) is printed by permission of Bloomsbury Publishing Plc on behalf of Michael Rosen. Every effort has been made to secure permission for the use of copyrighted material. If notified of any omission, the editor and publisher will gladly make the necessary correction in future printings.

Thanks also to L'Harmattan, publishers of *Destin à Part, seul déporté rescapé de la rafle de Clans du 5 octobre 1943* by Henry Bily; **Les Archives de la**

Vendée; Robert Laffont, publishers of *J'ai pas pleuré* by Ida Grinspan and Bertrand Poirot-Delpech; **Geste éditions**, publishers of *Les Chemins de la honte, Itinéraire d'une persécution, Deux-Sèvres 1940-44* by Jean-Marie Pouplain; **Klarsfeld**, publishers of *Le Memorial de la Déportation des Juifs de France* by Serge Klarsfeld; **Éditions Les Chantuseries**, publishers of *La trace, Le Destin des juifs de Vendée pendant laseconde guerre mondiale* by Louis Gouraud; **Éditions du centre**, publishers of *Jews Under the Italian Occupation* by Leon Poliakov and Jacques Sabille; and the online publication of "Récit de Philippe Glanzberg".

And special thanks to: **Nadia Hassani** for translating the letters from Oscar and Stella; **Teddy Rosen** for sharing the discoveries of the letters and photos; **Professor Helen Weinstein** and **HistoryWorks**, Cambridge, for their work for Holocaust Memorial Day, my work with them in schools and Helen's comments on this book; **Associate Professor Andy Pearce** from The UCL Centre for Holocaust Education, for reading the manuscript and being so generous with his time; **Nicola Wetherall MBE** from The UCL Centre for Holocaust Education for her help; **The Wiener Library** for their archive of Holocaust documents, and for the photo in this book; **The American Jewish Historical Society**, New England Archives; **Mémorial de la Shoah**, Paris; **Gerald Dardart**, historian of the Ardennes during the Second World War; my French teachers, especially **Keith** and the late **Thelma Emmans** at Watford Boys Grammar School; **Caroline Royds** who championed this book from the beginning; the late **Ted Rosen** and **Olga Rosen**; **Michael** and **Grant Rechnic**; and the late **Harold** and **Connie Rosen**, my parents, for telling me what they knew and didn't know.

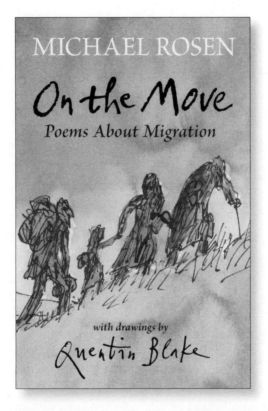

The following is an extract from *On the Move*, a collection
by Michael Rosen with drawings by Quentin Blake,
including the book's introduction and the poem
"Finding Out".

Migrant Poetry

Poetry is the migrant: it travels.
Poetry is the witness: it listens.
Poetry is the survivor: it lasts.

Migration is the story of the human race. Everything we know about history, from the fossil record through to today, shows us that human beings keep moving from place to place.

Sometimes it's for work and sometimes it's for education, but often it's because people have had to escape from where they were living before. They might have woken up to find that their country has changed overnight; perhaps invaded by another country's army, forcing them to run for their lives.

Without warning, they must travel however they can: by foot or by car, by train or by boat, to try to find safety. You may have seen photos of people making journeys like this on TV – especially, of the millions of men, women and children forced to leave Syria in recent years.

These people are "refugees". You might have heard the words "refugees" and "migrants" being used as if they mean the same thing, but it's important to know the difference.

"Migrants" are people who travel to find a better life – and who could return without a direct threat to their lives, though it might be to poor conditions. "Refugees" are people who have been forced to leave their homes, and would be in great danger if they tried to go back.

Some people speak about refugees and migrants as if they're bad or dangerous. They seem to think that "normal people" would never find themselves at the wrong place at the wrong time, needing to find a safe place to be.

But migration isn't just something that "happens to other people". If you look into your own family history, no matter where you come from, chances are that you will arrive at the story of your relatives' migration to where you live now.

From the time I was a boy, I knew that people

were missing from my own family history – aunts and uncles, who had been there before the Second World War, but weren't there after. And knowing they were gone was linked to a feeling that it would be impossible to find out what happened to them.

I did know that my aunts and uncles were Jewish, like my family living in London. And, as a teenager, I found out that the party in power in Germany during the war – the Nazis – had organized the murder of six million Jewish people, in what is now known as "The Holocaust".

But not only did the Nazis want to "remove" people: they wanted to remove all memory of them, any trace that they ever existed. They wanted my relatives to be wiped from European history.

When I found that out, I was determined to find out what happened. I was determined to remember them.

I've been writing poems about my family history, and migration, for a long time. Poetry is a way of thinking; it gives me a space to talk about things that are personal to me, but it also lets me leave things hanging in the air... To ask questions without giving too-neat answers.

On the Move gathers these poems together for the first time, and I've divided them into four sections.

In the first, there are poems about growing up as part of a Polish-Jewish family in London. The second explores how I came to know about the Second World War – which leads into the third section, telling the story of my "missing" relatives. After these very personal poems, I wanted the last section to connect up our experiences with migration around the world.

You also have Quentin Blake's extraordinary pictures to look at. They're "moving" in a different sort of way; I feel moved by the atmosphere they conjure up: the sense of people in danger sticking together, moving on and on.

These pictures could be people throughout history – on the move during the Second World War, or on the move today ... because our governments still turn away people with nowhere else to go;

because people still "disappear" on dangerous, difficult journeys.

I hope this book shows how we can reach out to each other, and share what it is that makes us human. I believe that we are, all of us, citizens of the world, and it seems to me that "home" shouldn't be decided by country borders.

Home is where you find it.

Michael Rosen

Finding Out

For years I tried to find out
what happened to my father's uncles.
All I had were scraps, words, names,
floating in front of me like leaves
falling off trees:
Oscar, Martin, Metz, route de Thionville,
Dentist, clockmender...

One day, my cousin in America wrote:
a distant relative had died.
In his papers
there were two letters
from one of the uncles, Oscar,
and two letters
from his sister in Poland, Stella,
all written during the war
and asking for help.

I pored over the letters
trying to give the words
a voice that I could hear.

Now that I had addresses,
the internet
and books
and museums
were kinder,
they gave me more and more.
Now I could make maps:
where the uncles went,
where they ran to,
where they hid,
where they were seized and taken to.

Then, one day, another email
arrived from my cousin in America.
His father and step-mother had died
and he had just been in the house.

"I noticed there was a closet," he said.
"It was locked, so I opened it. I could see
it was full of photos. There was a sealed-up box
in there. On the box, it said, 'Family Photos'.

I cut it open and inside there were old black
and white photos with names on them:
Oscar and Martin.
And many more.
They've been there for years and years.
I'll send them to you right now."
And he did.

Now I could see Oscar and Martin.
I could see their faces
and what Oscar looked like
in his First World War Army uniform.
There were more places, like Bielitz,
more names of brothers and sisters,
and photos of their father and mother.
These were my great grandparents
in New York
over a hundred years ago!

Pictures I had never seen.
Pictures my father had never seen…

"But why," I said to my cousin in America,
"was the closet locked?
Why were the photos in a sealed-up box?"

I had sat in that room with the closet
behind me and I had asked his father
about Oscar and Martin,
what did he know?

And all the time the photos were sitting
just a few feet away.
And all he had been able to give me were
falling leaves.